THE MYSTERIOUS ELEMENT

PAM ROBSON

Illustrated by Biz Hull

MACDONALD YOUNG BOOKS

Full steam ahead

We're going to Paris... we're going to Paris... the wheels of the train seemed to say, as they ate up the miles of track. Maria Sklodowska sat huddled on her stool in a fourth class carriage. She had been on the train for three days and Warsaw was now far behind her. "I'm going to Paris," she smiled. Paris meant freedom! Freedom to study science.

Maria shuffled uncomfortably. The cold, ladies-only carriage did not have proper seats. Only first-class passengers could travel in comfort; they had coal-fired boxes for warmth. Maria tucked her blanket around her cold feet. But her grey eyes sparkled.

At last her dream was coming true.

Dawn was breaking as the train approached Paris. She folded the blanket, pushed a stray fair curl beneath her hat and peered through the grimy windows. At last the train whooshed and gasped its way beneath the glass roof
of the station.

Spotted with soot, tired and nervous, Maria thought longingly of her family in Warsaw. Then she was almost jerked off her feet as the train stopped. She bunched her skirts and stepped down, a small, determined young woman. She had come to Paris to enrol as a student of chemistry and physics at the Sorbonne university. Waiting to meet her was her new brother-in-law.

"Maria?" A young gentleman raised his top hat and smiled.

"Kazimierz!" The two shook hands. Maria relaxed, it was comforting to hear a Polish voice.

"Are you too tired to walk to the apartment?"

"Oh no! I can't wait to see Paris." Maria took her brother-in-law's arm.

Outside, the early autumn sun coloured the tree-lined avenues. Soon she smelled baking bread and hot coffee. Wagons and carts rumbled by. Factory workers hurried past. "Here we are, Maria. Our apartment is on the second floor." Sighing with happiness, Maria followed Kazimierz up the stairs.

"I must enrol today," she announced firmly at breakfast the next morning. Kazimierz laughed at her eagerness.

Later that afternoon Maria stood outside the Sorbonne. She watched as students hurried by, talking quickly to each other, and noticed that there were only a few women.

Taking a deep breath, Maria marched through the doors, found the registrar and began the business of enrolling at the university. At last, the registrar said, "Please sign here," and she wrote her new French name, 'Mademoiselle Marie Sklodowska'.

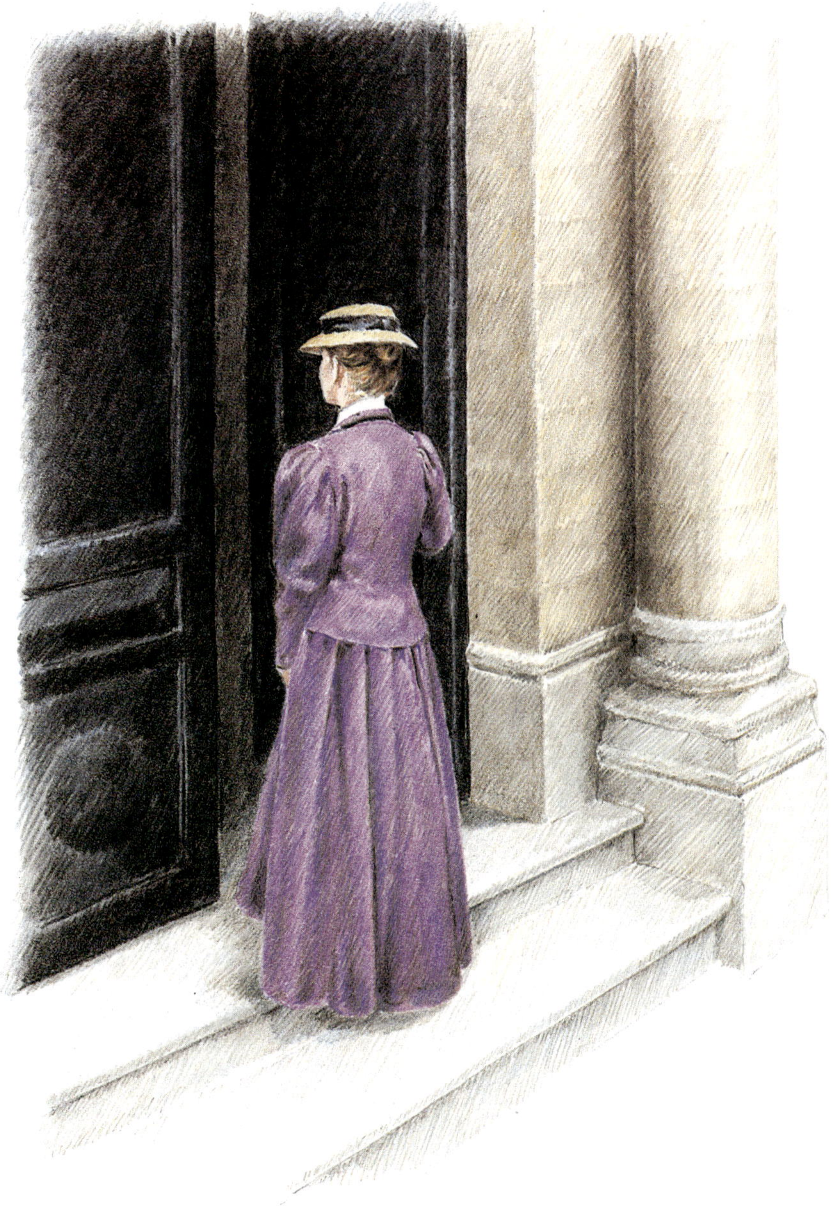

Radishes for lunch

Each morning Marie had to make the hour-long journey to the Sorbonne on a horse-drawn omnibus. But she became tired of all this travelling and after six months she rented an attic room close to the Sorbonne.

Every day she worked in the half-built science laboratories, where the students discussed the very latest scientific discoveries. Marie found it much easier to understand French now.

"Monsieur Pasteur's work sounds so exciting!" she declared to her friend Jadwiga.

At night, while the male students had fun in the noisy boulevard cafés, Marie read alone in her room by the light of an oil lamp. She was too busy studying for her science degree to go out and enjoy herself.

Her tiny
sixth floor room
had only one window.
In winter it was so cold that the water in her jug froze. One freezing night she piled all her belongings and even a chair on top of the bed just to keep warm.

One day when Marie opened her food cupboard she found nothing there but radishes. "Oh well," she shrugged, "radishes for lunch." Later that day she fainted from hunger. When she told Kazimierz, who was a doctor, he was horrified. Marie studied so hard that she often forgot to do everyday things like shopping and eating.

But all this hard work paid off. It took Marie just two years to pass her degree, and she was the top student! She hurried back to Poland to visit her family. "We are so proud of you," said her father delightedly.

Before long Marie was awarded a scholarship. This was wonderful – now she would have money to live on and the opportunity to study again.

So she eagerly returned to Paris.

Marie Curie

"If only I had a bigger laboratory to work in," grumbled Marie to her Polish friends, the Kowalskis. She desperately needed more room for her studies.

"I know someone who might be able to solve your problem," said Mr Kowalski thoughtfully. "His name is Pierre Curie – he works nearby."

Pierre was a science teacher who also loved to study in his run-down laboratory. His invention of a sensitive machine which could measure tiny electric charges was to be vital in Marie's future work.

Although Pierre was only 35 years old, he was already a respected scientist. "He looks so young and serious," Marie thought when she first saw him. They spent many hours together talking about science and soon fell in love. They were married in 1895, a year after Marie passed her mathematics degree.

Radioactivity

"Pierre, Monsieur Becquerel has discovered something odd about uranium. He claims that it gives off rays powerful enough to leave marks on photographic plates!" announced Marie.

Pierre wrinkled his brow. "How could that be?" he said thoughtfully.

Quite by accident, Henri Becquerel had found that uranium gave off mysterious invisible rays. He had actually discovered what is now known as radioactivity.

Marie couldn't stop thinking about Becquerel's rays – there was a mystery here that she wanted to solve. She thought carefully about what she already knew.

Her science studies had shown Marie that everything in the world is made up of different substances called elements. Iron, lead, copper and even oxygen are all elements. Most elements are very stable; they never change. But radioactive elements, such as uranium, are very unstable. When uranium grows older, it gives off tiny radioactive particles and very, very slowly changes into lead.

The Curies were not rich and although they loved to study they had to earn money to live. So Marie trained to become a teacher at a girls' school. Then she found that she was expecting a baby and in the autumn, Irene was born.

However, Marie continued to study. She longed to become a doctor of science, but to achieve that she must study a subject that no one had ever looked at before. And she knew exactly what to choose – Becquerel's rays!

"I am determined to find the answer to this puzzle!" she declared.

So, in a freezing cold, ramshackle laboratory, with only a few wooden worktables and a rickety chair, Marie and Pierre began to search for the truth about the mysterious rays.

"I will test other substances," Marie decided. "Perhaps uranium is not the only element to produce these rays of energy."

Using Pierre's Piezoelectric Quartz Balance, she could work out how much energy different elements gave off. First she tested uranium and measured the strong rays that it gave off. Next she tested thorium and found that it gave off stronger rays. Then she decided to test pitchblende.

Pitchblende is a mineral which contains uranium. To her surprise, Marie found that it produced much stronger rays than uranium. She was puzzled. The only explanation could be that pitchblende contained another energy-producing element apart from uranium. But what could it be?

It must be a completely new element!

"We must find out what it is," said Marie and got ready for some hard work.

Steaming cauldrons

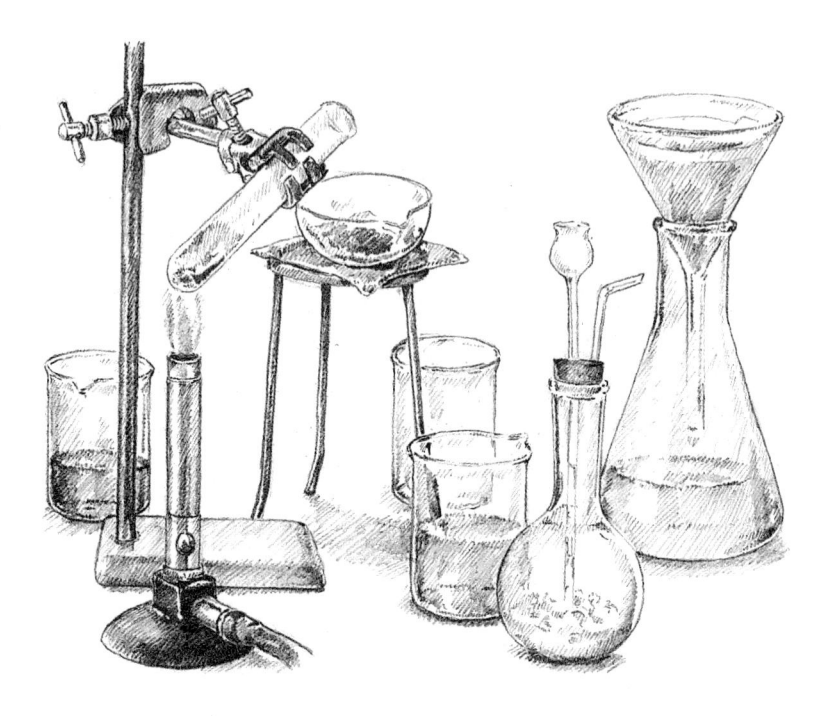

"Let's try breaking down the pitchblende with chemicals," said Marie. But the results were disappointing.

"Why not try distilling it?" suggested Gustave Bémont, another scientist. This time the results were better. Even stronger rays were produced. "I think there are two new elements here!" Marie gasped.

A few months later they were able to name one of them. "I think we should call it polonium," Marie declared, "after my country."

That summer Marie and Pierre reported that polonium gave off rays which were four hundred times stronger than uranium.

The rays showed that uranium, thorium and polonium were all radioactive.

One morning a letter arrived for Pierre. "Marie, listen to this! You've been awarded the Prix Gegner. You're to receive 3800 francs!"

Marie smiled to herself – important letters were usually sent to a woman's husband, even when they concerned the woman herself. "Do you think they will write and tell *me*?" she joked.

They still had to separate the new elements from the rest of the pitchblende. But for the next three months it was the holidays and time to take a break.

By the end of November Marie was finally able to say triumphantly, "There *is* another new element, look at this reading! Its rays are the strongest I've ever seen – they are nine hundred times stronger than uranium!" She wrote in her notebook the name 'radium'.

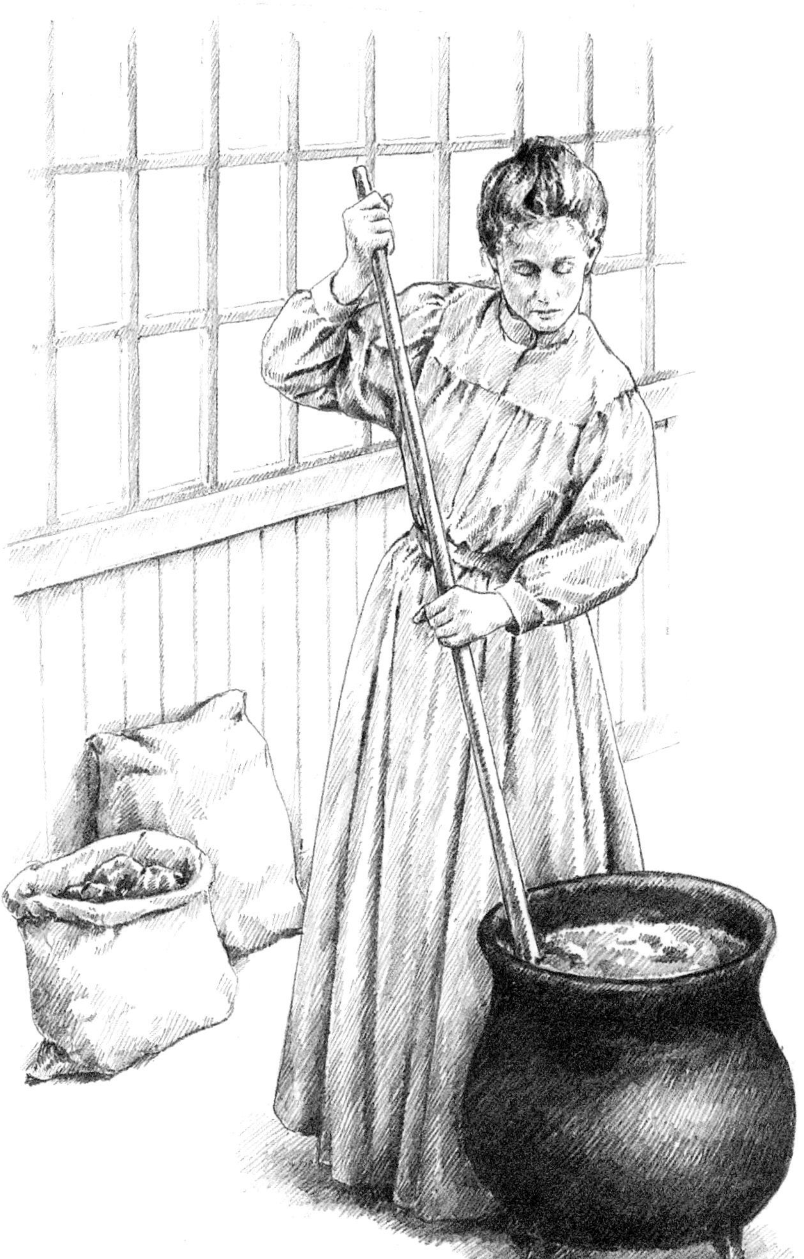

The following spring she took on the enormous task of separating radium from pitchblende. Pierre turned his attention to finding out more about the mysterious rays of energy. They decided to give the strange energy a name – radioactivity.

Sacks containing tonnes of pitchblende – brown dust mixed with pine needles – had been delivered all the way from a country called Bohemia.

Now they needed an even bigger laboratory for their work. Pierre and Marie chose a large shed with a leaking, glass roof, worn pine tables, a blackboard and an old cast-iron stove. "At least we can make some tea when the weather is cold," she declared.

For hour after hour, Marie stirred huge cauldrons full of hot pitchblende with an iron bar almost as big as herself. The liquids that she made filled dozens of small containers.

The glow of success

"I *will* do it," she declared grimly. "I *know* there's radium in this pitchblende." She coughed loudly. "I do wish the air wasn't always so full of dust, though. But we will find our new elements." She loved the challenge facing her.

Although she was deeply involved in her research into radium, Marie also enjoyed teaching. She was well liked and her students always waited at the classroom window to see their favourite teacher arrive. Then they would rush to their seats, ready for an exciting lesson for Marie was able to make science as fascinating to them as it was to her.

One warm summer's evening, Pierre and Marie made an astonishing discovery. As they visited their laboratory, the creaky door swung open. Spellbound, they gazed at the mysterious glow before them.

A strange blue light shone from the glass containers of liquid. "You hoped there might be colour in our new elements, Pierre!" Marie exclaimed. Never in their wildest dreams had they imagined that their discovery would give out its own light.

They were now close to success, but Marie and Pierre were both beginning to feel unwell. Marie was losing weight. "I feel so tired," she complained, "but I cannot rest when there is so much to do."

Marie and Pierre did not realize how dangerous the rays could be. Radium was beautiful, but it was also a powerful and deadly new element.

The Nobel Prize

Then at last came the day the Curies had been working towards. As Marie held up a tiny container, she knew this was it! The result of all their hard work was one-tenth of a gram of pure radium.

Marie invited her students from Sevres and her sister Bronia to watch her receive her doctorate for her work on Becquerel's rays. Marie had to answer questions on her amazing research and on the discovery of the two new elements: radium and polonium.

"Isn't Madame wonderful!" the students sighed, amazed and delighted to see a woman achieve success in the world of science. That night, in a friend's garden, Pierre proudly demonstrated the glow from a tube of their radium. It was a wonderful end to the day.

At the end of 1903, the Curies and Henri Becquerel were awarded the Nobel Prize. But some newspapers claimed, "Madame Curie only helped her husband in his work." They were unwilling to believe that a woman could be a scientist.

Though they had achieved worldwide fame, the Curies remained dedicated to their research. Pierre had to write to the Swedish Academy, "We will be unable to attend the award ceremony. Madame Curie is unwell, and we cannot take time off from our work." This simple modesty was typical of them. "Radium does not belong to us," they insisted, "it is for the world."

Epilogue

On a wet day in Paris, in 1906, Pierre died tragically, knocked down by a horse-drawn wagon. Marie overcame her grief and continued her work alone. Despite her poor health, which was growing worse, she travelled to America and Britain and attended international conferences.

Marie Curie's greatest achievements were the discovery of radium and the fact that radioactivity came from the atom. Because of her precise scientific work, and her determination to succeed, doctors can now treat and even cure cancer, archaeologists can tell the age of ancient objects and nuclear power is used to produce electricity. Sadly, the discovery has also led to the destructive power of nuclear weapons.

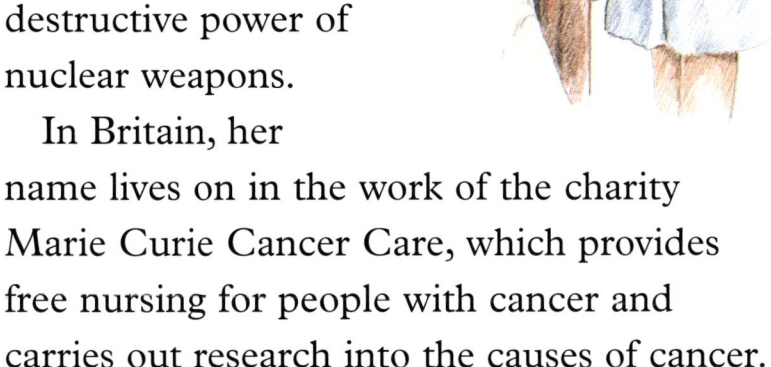

In Britain, her name lives on in the work of the charity Marie Curie Cancer Care, which provides free nursing for people with cancer and carries out research into the causes of cancer.

Timeline

Marie Curie was born on 7 November 1867 in Warsaw, Poland.

1891	Marie leaves Poland and enrols at the Sorbonne University in Paris.
1895	Marie marries Pierre Curie.
1895	Wilhelm Röntgen discovers X-rays.
1896	Henri Becquerel discovers the radioactivity of uranium.
1897	The Curies' daughter, Irene, is born.
1898	The Curies discover a new element – they name it polonium.
1899	Marie begins the task of finding another new element – radium.
1902	Marie isolates one decigram of radium.
1903	Marie and Pierre Curie and Henri Becquerel win the Nobel Prize for Physics.
1906	Pierre Curie is killed in a tragic accident.
1910	The standard unit of measurement of radioactivity – the curie – is set up.

1911   Marie Curie wins the Nobel Prize for Chemistry.

1914   Marie organizes mobile X-ray units during World War One.

1932   Scientists split the atom. The geiger counter is invented to measure radiation.

1934   Irene and Frederic Curie-Joliot discover artificial radioactivity.

1942   The first nuclear reactor is set up in Chicago, USA.

1945   Atomic bombs are dropped on Japan.

1962   Cobalt-60, an artificial radioactive substance, is used to treat cancer.

Marie Curie died on 4 July 1934 in France. She was 66 years old.

Glossary

atom	the tiniest particle of an element that can take part in a chemical reaction
cancer	this disease affects cells in the body – radiation treatment, called radiotherapy, can kill cancer cells
curie	the 'curie' is a measure of radioactivity
element	everything in the world is made up of different mixtures of elements
nuclear physics	the area of science which studies the atom and what is inside it
Piezoelectric Quartz Balance	a machine which measures tiny amounts of electricity
radiation	energy in the form of rays given out from the atom
radioactivity	when some elements break up and give off radiation
x-rays	these are used to photograph bones inside our bodies